Railscene

SUNDE

The Photographs of Ian S. Carr

Dedicated to my parents -
the late Thomas and Ruth Carr -
and to the young people of Tyne and
Wear whom I have taught or otherwise
tried to help on the journey through life.

Ian S. Carr

AUTHOR'S ACKNOWLEDGEMENTS

Apart from University days in London in the 1950s, I have spent most of my life in the North East. During that time I have had the opportunity to put on photographic record countless railway scenes, many now gone forever.

I am well aware that my pursuit of this task would have been more difficult, perhaps unachievable, without the help of numerous railway employees and enthusiasts. Over the years they have enabled me to secure some elusive and now treasured pictures for which I am deeply grateful.

For permission to photograph on their properties, I am also indebted to the British Railways Board, National Coal Board/British Coal, Doxford & Sunderland and the Port of Sunderland Authority.

Thanks are due to Neil Sinclair, author of *Railways of Sunderland,* for assistance with the historical background to my book and to Alan Lister of Tyne and Wear Museums for his help in finalising the selection of photographs.

Ian S. Carr
Sunderland
1999

FOREWORD

The increasing significance of road transport, coupled with the decline and closure of heavy industries in and around Sunderland, has resulted in a drastic diminution of the rail network in recent years. Today freight customers are confined to the South Dock Branch, although on the passenger side the Sunderland to Newcastle service is more intensive than ever before. The Leamside route survives intact but has been mothballed since 1991.

This book presents images of those railways and their surroundings from the mid-1950s, when coal and shipbuilding dominated the area, to the present day. The fact that the pictures are all in the Sunderland area clearly illustrates the wealth of railway history that the City has to offer.

Ian Carr, a rail passenger for some sixty years, is well-known for his photographic contributions to national railway magazines, and his work has appeared in some two hundred books. He has been involved in several one-man photographic exhibitions at museums.

Ian was Founder Honorary Secretary of Monkwearmouth Station Museum Association, which later became the North Tyneside Steam Railway Association.

We are very grateful to him for allowing us publishing access to his unique photographic collection and for giving his ongoing enthusiastic support to Tyne and Wear Museums.

Councillor Barney Rice, JP
Chair Tyne and Wear Museums Joint Committee

Councillor Ralph Baxter
Vice-Chair Tyne and Wear Museums Joint Committee

Dr. David Fleming, OBE
Director, Tyne and Wear Museums

RAILSCENES AROUND SUNDERLAND

CONTENTS

RAILSCENES AROUND SUNDERLAND

INTRODUCTION

Sunderland has enjoyed a rich and diverse railway heritage ranging from wooden wagonways taking coal to keel boats on the River Wear in the 1700s, through colliery lines using stationary engines, self-acting inclines and steam locomotives to present-day diesel multiple units, locomotives, HSTs and occasionally diverted GNER electrics. When I started photographing in 1955 it was impossible to go far in Sunderland without hearing or seeing evidence of a railway. The view of the network of lines seen from a prominent spot such as Penshaw Hill was impressive.

However, as far as traction was concerned, even at that time transition was underway. Diesel multiple units were taking over from steam on Newcastle- Middlesbrough services, a North British Locomotive Co. diesel was in evidence on the NCB's Hetton Colliery Railway - while further afield the prototype Deltic was undergoing trials. One has to accept that successive generations of folk have been nurtured not only on the steam locomotive but on other types of traction as well; indeed for many present-day car owners the railway itself may seem to be something of an anachronism.

Forty years of economic change have seen heavy industries such as coal, coke, iron and steel and shipbuilding swept away and accordingly the rail network has shrunk in sympathy. Today the Newcastle-Middlesbrough coast route is the main survivor in Sunderland with a 15 minute daytime passenger service between Tyneside and Wearside subsidised by Nexus. In the 1950s, Sunderland benefited from through trains to places such as York, Leeds, Manchester, Bristol, Colchester and London. These ran via Hartlepool and some included restaurant cars.
Even Middlesbrough trains once boasted buffet cars - a facility later perpetuated by minibuffets on certain dmus. A 1996 innovation put Sunderland on the TransPennine network with through trains to Liverpool mostly via Newcastle and Durham.

At Ryhope Grange Junction the now singled South Dock branch leaves the coast route; it serves Petrofina plc and also sees miscellaneous traffic such as coal, aluminium and chipboard. At the waterfront the Port of Sunderland Authority's line is the last industrial railway in the city. The NER's 'old main line' through Fencehouses and Washington via the Victoria Bridge has been mothballed south of Wardley for normal traffic since 1991. Apart from these lines and the preserved Bowes Railway, shared with Gateshead, every other working railway in Sunderland has vanished. I am only too aware of the numerous 'last' pictures that I have taken over the years.

Railway photography nowadays can be more difficult than it used to be. Lineside photographic permits were withdrawn in 1977 and railways subjected to stringent Health and Safety conditions. Other problems include the increased speed of trains, prolific lineside vegetation, high bridge parapets, security fencing, advertising hoardings and new buildings. The awarding of rail franchises to private companies means that it is harder to acquire information about train workings - which could happily have been gleaned from the Area Manager of yesteryear.

This book features most types of traction and looks at Sunderland's railways by route rather than by theme. A potted history appears in the Section Headings. Special attention is paid to the area around Monkwearmouth Station which first opened in 1848 and celebrated its 150th anniversary on 19 June 1998.

It is hoped that the book will provide enjoyment for those already interested in railways and arouse curiosity amongst a wider public who may like to compare some of the older views with what exists on the ground at the same location today.

IAN S. CARR

1. LAMBTON RAILWAY

In the early 19th century several collieries which were later served by the Lambton system, such as North Biddick and Newbottle, were connected by wagonways to the River Wear where coal was put into keel boats to be taken downriver to waiting seagoing vessels. In 1815 the Nesham family abandoned their earlier staiths in favour of a railway from Newbottle to staiths at Sunderland utilising stationary engines and horses; this obviated the need for coal transhipment.

In 1822 the line was purchased by J. G. Lambton who linked it to his Lambton and Lumley wagonways. The Newbottle Railway's route was altered between Philadelphia and Grindon in 1835 and it was now carrying coal from collieries developed between Fencehouses and Sherburn. After the opening of the Penshaw Branch railway in 1852/3 colliery trains obtained running powers over NER metals to the staiths end of the Newbottle Wagonway via Millfield curve. From 1865 access was had to Lambton Staiths via the Deptford Branch; the Newbottle line was then progressively abandoned.

Philadelphia became the hub of one of the largest colliery systems in the North-East. Its locomotive shed had a very considerable allocation and engines were repaired or rebuilt at the adjacent Lambton Engine Works. Workings over BR lines are featured in the section on the Penshaw Branch.

Contraction of the Lambton system began in the 1960s with closure of several collieries and NCB workings over the Penshaw branch ceased in 1967. The line to Houghton closed in 1975, that to Philadelphia and Herrington in 1985 and the final section from Penshaw Yard to Lambton Coke Works in 1986.

1.1

Remains of the wooden 4ft 2in. gauge wagonway excavated at the site of Lambton Cokeworks, Fencehouses, and believed to date from about 1780. Photographed on 29 March 1996.

1.2

Nesham's 1815 wagonway from Newbottle to staiths at Sunderland via the Grindon Hills passed through what was to become Bishopwearmouth Cemetery. The bridge at the Farnham Terrace entrance which carried the railway dated from about 1855. It was demolished when the cemetery entrance was levelled shortly after this picture was taken on 13 May 1965.

1.3
Outside the Lambton Engine Works, for many years, stood the preserved remains of Hackworth 0-6-0 locomotive BRADDYLL seen here on 16 April 1973. The engine was built for the South Hetton Colliery about 1837 and now reposes at Shildon's Timothy Hackworth Museum.

1.4
With the rundown of local mineral railways, Lambton Engine Works at Philadelphia began to overhaul engines from far afield. This quintet, photographed near Herrington Colliery on 14 April 1980, included ex-works South Wales diesel 522/2010, in dark blue livery, which was presumably soon to return home on a low-loader.

1.5
NCB 0-6-0ST 51 (RSH 7101/1943)
approaches Philadelphia with a coal train
from Herrington Colliery to Penshaw
Yard. On the right is 0-6-0ST 58
(VF 5299/1945) which formerly worked
at the staiths end of the Hetton Colliery
Railway. 18 April 1968.

1.6
The tumbledown condition of one of
Philadelphia's sheds on 6 June 1970.
From left to right are NCB 0-6-2T 29
(Kitson 4263/1904), 5 (RS 3377/1909)
and 52 (Neilson Reid 5408/1899)- all of
which have been preserved. Note the NCB
brakevan, one of several used for
journeys over BR metals.

1.7

Having been purchased by the Lambton No. 29 Locomotive Syndicate for use on the North Yorkshire Moors Railway, the 0-6-2T has its NCB identity removed outside Philadelphia shed on 18 June 1970. The picture shows to good effect the rounded cab.

1.8

Preserved A4 4-6-2 LNER 4498 SIR NIGEL GRESLEY attracts the crowds as it arrives for a few years residence at the NCB shed, Philadelphia, on 31 July 1968.

1.9
NCB diesel 506 (ex-BR D9504) is seen at Bank Top, Philadelphia, with a coal train from Houghton Colliery to Penshaw Yard on 27 August 1971. The relatively modern locomotive contrasts with the wooden-bodied wagons.

1.10
Seldom figuring in photographs was this 0-4-0 electric loco (RSH 7804/1954). It spent its life in the bowels of Lambton Coke Works, moving its coking car along the few yards of track between the coke ovens and the quencher, where water was sprayed onto the inferno, giving rise to clouds of condensing steam.
12 August 1970.

1.11
NCB 0-6-2T 31 (Kitson 4533/1907) trundles past Burnmoor Crossing, near Shiney Row, with a few coal wagons for Penshaw Yard on 25 August 1967. With the cessation of workings over BR metals earlier in the year, these locomotives were confined to the NCB internal system.

1.12
NCB 507 (ex-BR D9525) and BR 6912 (later Class 37) contemplate one another in Penshaw Yard on 23 August 1973. Close to the former Penshaw Station, the yard was the focal point for transfer of traffic between the NCB Lambton system and BR. Penshaw Yard eventually closed in 1986.

2. HETTON COLLIERY RAILWAY

The 1822 eight mile Hetton Colliery Railway over Warden Law linked Hetton Colliery with staiths at Sunderland and was of national significance as the first complete line engineered by George Stephenson. It used locomotives on the level stretches with stationary engines and self-acting inclines elsewhere. The Lambton Collieries Company took over the Hetton Coal Company in 1911.

Probably the doyen of north-east mineral railways, the HCR has tended to receive less than its fair share of publicity. The major part of the line closed on 9 September 1959.

2.1
On the relatively level stretch at the
Hetton end of the 1822 Hetton Colliery
Railway, outside cylinder 0-6-0T 41 (Kerr
Stuart 3074/1917) was pictured at
Three Tuns crossing on 27 August
1959, a few weeks before closure.

2.2
View from Copt Hill down the stationary
engine-worked incline to Hetton Dene.
The three-rail system was used above
the passing loops on inclines, thereafter
it was single track. The signalbox is at
the crossing of the Houghton to
Seaham road. The trackwork would
present a challenge to modellers!

2.3
View along the Copt Hill stationary engine-worked Flat to the foot of Warden Law Bank. Wagons were then hauled to the summit of the line by the Warden Law stationary engine whose chimney is visible in the right background.
26 August 1959.

2.4
Warden Law stationary engine house and the summit of the Hetton Colliery Railway, some 600 feet above sea-level.
April 1959.

2.5
From Warden Law the HCR descended to North Moor by four self-acting inclines on which downgoing loaded wagons pulled up the empties. This 1959 view from the Stoneygate to Ryhope road on No. 1 incline looks towards Warden Law. A wagon is stabled in the loop at a nearby coal depot.

2.6
Empty wagons approach the 'kip' at the top of No. 2 self-acting incline.
The descending loaded wagons used the tracks on either side. August 1959.

2.7
A sad scene at the foot of No. 4 incline at North Moor on 11 September 1959. Following closure of the section from Hetton, NCB 0-4-0ST 38 (RSH 7756/1953) had dragged the last length of rope from the four self-acting inclines for cutting up. How many of these goodly souls are alive today? Note the cloth caps!

2.8
On the connecting line between the HCR and Silksworth Colliery (opened in the 1920's after the Lambton & Hetton Company purchased Silksworth Colliery from the Marquis of Londonderry), NCB Hunslet 0-4-0 diesel hydraulic 157 (6676/1967) heads empty wagons from Hylton Road Coal Depot for South Dock on 30 July 1970. The short section of the HCR from Hylton Road was kept open for this traffic until June 1972. Tunstall Hills are in the background.

2.9
On a murky day in 1957, NCB 0-6-0 diesel hydraulic No. 1 (North British Locomotive Co. 27410/1955) approaches Ranson Street, between Eden Vale and Durham Road Tunnel, with empty wagons from the staiths.

2.10
NCB 0-6-0DE 514 (ex-BR 12084) crosses Chester Road bridge with coal empties from Hylton Road Coal Depot to South Dock via Silksworth on 1 June 1972, a few days before this final portion of the HCR closed.

2.11
Plaque erected at the landscaped area where the HCR formerly crossed the BR Penshaw Branch.

2.12
A former Taff Vale Railway locomotive, NCB 0-6-2T 52 nears the HCR bridge over the Penshaw line with empty coal wagons from Hylton Road Coal Depot and probably the power station on 20 April 1959. On the left the HCR descends to the tunnel under Hylton Road on its way to the staiths. Note the disused signal. This entire area is now landscaped. No. 52 is preserved at the Keighley & Worth Valley Railway.

2.13
On 26 August 1964 at Lambton Staiths NCB 0-4-0ST 39 (RSH 7757/1953) takes water outside the shed while 35 (Hawthorn Leslie 3024/1913) shunts on the right. The left-hand tunnel leads to Deptford Junction and the right-hand serves the Hetton Colliery line. The local NCB engines had rounded cabs to negotiate these tunnels. Traffic from the Hetton line was dealt with at Lambton Staiths during the railway's final years.

3. FENCEHOUSES TO FOLLINGSBY (OLD MAIN LINE)

The Durham Junction Railway opened in 1838 for freight and in 1840 for passengers from Rainton Meadows to join the Stanhope & Tyne line at Washington. It included the Victoria Bridge over the Wear and was intended as a through North to South route but the Newcastle and Darlington Junction Railway to Rainton was only opened in 1844.
A shorter route than the S & T for trains to Newcastle, from Washington to Pelaw via Usworth, was opened to goods in 1849 and passengers in 1850, this forming part of the NER's main line from Newcastle to Darlington - a function which it lost in 1872 when the main line through the Team Valley opened. The 'old main line', however, saw extensive use for diversions when the ECML was being repaired, these sometimes being of such duration as to merit inclusion in the public timetable. Passenger services between Pelaw and Penshaw were withdrawn in 1963 and south of Penshaw in 1964. The old main line, sometimes known as the Leamside line, is intact today but has seen no regular through traffic south of Wardley since 1991.

3.1
A4 4-6-2 60028 WALTER K. WHIGHAM was photographed from the station footbridge at Fencehouses as it headed a diverted King's Cross to Edinburgh train in 1959. The signal box had a double overhang - over the NCB lines on the left as well as the BR route.

3.2
A3 4-6-2 60042 SINGAPORE passes Wapping Bridge (near Burnmoor, and the end of the four track section from Penshaw North) with a diverted Edinburgh to King's Cross train on 18 June 1961.

3.3
40086 is seen at Penshaw with a train lifting the limestone siding and relaying it at a higher level on a bitter cold 13 December 1975.

3.4
Hauled notionally by D186 (later Class 46) NCB 0-6-2T 29 passes the remains of Penshaw Station as it makes for Thornaby in June 1970. Along with No. 5 it is now at the North Yorkshire Moors Railway.

3.5
V2 2-6-2 60964 THE DURHAM LIGHT
INFANTRY approaches Penshaw North
with a freight heading towards
Washington and Pelaw on 2 August
1959.

3.6
Glinting in the afternoon sunshine, A4 4-6-2 60015 QUICKSILVER (one of the original Silver Jubilee quartet) approaches Penshaw North with a diverted northbound express on a Sunday in 1959. The NCB lines from Penshaw Yard to Cox Green Junction, complete with water columns, are on the left; the BR goods lines are in the centre.

3.7
Edinburgh Haymarket A4 4-6-2 60011 EMPIRE OF INDIA passes beneath the gantry-type Penshaw North signal box with a diverted train for King's Cross in 1959.

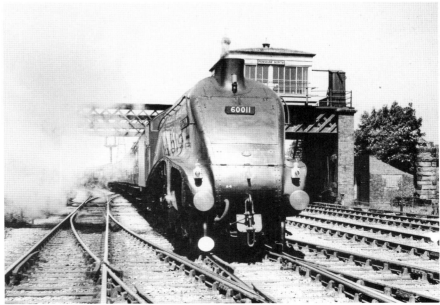

3.8
At Penshaw North, K1 2-6-0 62026 has
run round a freight from Sunderland
South Dock to the Consett line and is
about to leave for the Victoria Bridge on
31 August 1964. Note the wood-bodied
NCB Lambton wagons at the nearby coal
depot. Penshaw Monument is visible on
the hill in the background.

3.9

The Leamside route from Pelaw to Tursdale, the 'old main line', was closed and mothballed south of Wardley in May 1991. On a wet 23 June 1993, 37519 gingerly negotiates the rusted layout at Penshaw North as it heads south with a train recovering rail lengths following singling of parts of the line. The signal box and lines to Cox Green have gone.

3.10

Shower clouds cast shadows in the background as A4 4-6-2 60026 MILES BEEVOR approaches Penshaw North from Washington with a diverted Newcastle to King's Cross train in 1959. The line to Cox Green and Sunderland (Penshaw Branch) is on the right.

3.11
A4 4-6-2 60022 MALLARD crosses the Victoria Bridge with the 11.05 Newcastle to King's Cross train diverted on 19 July 1959. Note the check rails for the sharp curve round to Penshaw North.

3.12
D6762 (later Class 37) heads a northbound freight over the magnificent Victoria Bridge between Penshaw and Washington on 28 August 1964.

3.13
A Q6 0-8-0 and brakevan clatter across the Victoria Bridge over the River Wear between Washington and Penshaw on 28 August 1964. The Victoria Bridge was opened on Queen Victoria's Coronation Day in 1838.

3.14
Following reversal at Washington, 37216/164 make for the Victoria Bridge with Consett to Redcar iron ore empties that had travelled via the reinstated Biddick Lane line. 19 July 1975.

3.15
Schoolboys write in the grime on V3 2-6-2T 67689 as it pauses at Washington with the evening train to Newcastle on 14 September 1956. The sparsely filled spartan passenger service was used by employees from the nearby chemical works. Note the water column and lower quadrant signals. The youngsters should be aged about 50 today!

3.16
V2 2-6-2 60805 pounds over the level crossing at Usworth with a diverted northbound freight on 21 June 1959. Note the signal box with its single overhang, also the gas lighting and platelayers' trolley.

3.17
A4 4-6-2 60029 WOODCOCK heads
south through Usworth on the diverted
13.15 Edinburgh to King's Cross on
Sunday, 23 August 1959.

3.18
National Power 59201 VALE OF YORK (with bell) and 59203 VALE OF PICKERING doublehead a test train from Wardley Opencast Disposal Point on 9 August 1997. It was returning to a Yorkshire power station via Pelaw.

3.19
47380 about to leave Follingsby Freightliner Terminal with a train for Cardiff via Pelaw on 30 March 1987. The Terminal closed from 6 April of that year.

4. HARRATON TO THREE HORSE SHOES

This was part of the former Stanhope & Tyne Railway opened from Stanhope to South Shields for freight in 1834 and passengers in 1835. Following bankruptcy and suspension of services in 1841, the line was taken over by the Pontop and South Shields Railway. On Wearside passenger services east of Washington ceased in 1853, when the Penshaw to Fawcett Street line opened, and ceased west of Washington in 1869. These sections closed to freight in 1966 but the Washington to South Pelaw portion was reinstated for Redcar to Consett iron ore trains travelling via Leamside and Penshaw; this section finally closed in 1981.

4.1
Reclamation of small coal from the trackbed of the former Stanhope & Tyne line between Harraton and Biddick Lane on 12 August 1988. This was necessary to avoid any chance of spontaneous combustion taking place in the trackbed when it was upgraded to a public footpath and cycleway.

4.2
Tender-first 9F 2-10-0 92099 passes Biddick Lane with empty wagons for Penshaw from the South Pelaw area on 18 July 1966. This movement necessitated reversal at Washington

4.3

Looking woebegone and weary, Tyne Dock shed's 9F 2-10-0 92065 approaches the level crossing at Biddick Lane with an iron ore train for Consett on 18 July 1966.

4.4

The premises of Calders Ltd., Timber Merchants, Washington were situated between the Victoria Bridge and the Stanhope & Tyne line. A humble and seldom photographed rail travelling crane busies itself on 28 October 1970.

4.5
WD 2-8-0 90445 with the Stephenson Locomotive Society's East Durham Limited tour of 15 May 1965 is taking water at Washington on the Stanhope & Tyne line. It has travelled from Harton Junction via West Boldon and Barmston. The Leamside route parallelled the S & T hereabouts - it is beyond the cabins on the left.

4.6
Newalls Insulation & Chemical Co. Ltd., Washington, boasted this spotless 0-4-0 diesel hydraulic MARGARET (EEV D1126/1966). It was photographed near Chemical Works signal box on 28 October 1970.

4.7

D5182 (later Class 25) passes Three Horse Shoes with a Tyne Dock to Consett iron ore train on 26 August 1966. A banking engine would assist this heavy load on the severe gradients beyond South Pelaw. The S & T east of Washington had numerous level crossings, doubtless a factor in its closure.

5. PENSHAW NORTH TO SUNDERLAND CENTRAL, SOUTH DOCK AND THE DEPTFORD BRANCH

The Penshaw Branch opened from Penshaw to Hendon Junction for freight in 1852 and to Fawcett Street terminus for passengers in 1853, the latter station being in use until the opening of Sunderland Central in 1879. Fawcett Street's buildings then survived for another century until obliterated by construction of the Civic Centre.

The freight branch from Pallion to Deptford and Lambton Staiths opened in 1865. Colliery trains had running powers over NER/LNER/BR metals between Harraton Colliery, Penshaw, Lambton Staiths and South Dock. The staiths closed in January 1967.

Passenger services were withdrawn from Millfield in 1955 and from the remaining stations in 1964. The line from Fawcett Street Junction to Sunderland Central was severed in 1965. Freight services ceased between Penshaw and Hylton in 1967 and from Deptford and Pallion to Hendon Junction in 1984.

Much of the trackbed west of Fawcett Street has been infilled and landscaped to give a footpath/cycleway, but the railway will be reinstated in the event of a Metro extension to South Hylton.

5.1

Cox Green Junction was where NCB trains from Penshaw Yard joined the BR line from Penshaw North. Here Clayton D8601 heads a Tyne Yard to Pallion goods on 16 May 1967. The junction was fixed for BR lines only following the cessation of NCB traffic to the staiths earlier in the year.

5.2

NCB 0-6-2T 10 (RS 3378/1909) passes through Cox Green with coal for Lambton Staiths on 27 August 1965. The station lost its passenger service in 1964. The overbridge to the Wearside Golf Club can be seen in the distance.

5.3
G5 0-4-4T 67258 gets away from Cox Green with the 13.42 Durham to Sunderland train on 28 March 1957. A footpath between the fences on the right gave access to the golf course from the station.

5.4
A8 4-6-2T 69889 approaches Offerton Lane with the 13.42 Durham to Sunderland train on a snowy New Year's Day 1958.

5.6
Hylton signal box and level crossing photographed on 17 August 1967.

5.5
Milepost 2 from Penshaw North near the Hylton distant signal. Note PENSH'R on the post - an abbreviation for Pensher, the former spelling of the place name.
24 October 1967.

5.7
Construction of the present A19 road taking place over the former railway (closed to freight on this stretch in August 1967) west of Hylton on 22 August 1970.

5.8
Clayton D8601 having worked the 04.25 goods from Tyne Yard via South Dock is about to enter the lime-encrusted sidings at Ford Quarry, South Hylton, on 28 May 1970.

5.9
A wagon of coal descends the rope-worked incline to Ford Paper Mill, South Hylton, on a wintry 31 December 1970.

5.10

LMS design 4MT 2-6-0 43015 approaches Ford Works, between Hylton and Pallion, with the Summer Saturday Blackpool to South Shields train on 8 August 1959. The train travelled from Tebay via Ravenstonedale, Stainmore Summit, Evenwood, Brancepeth and Fencehouses.

5.11

V3 2-6-2T 67687 threads Claxheugh Rock Cutting with the 07.40 Middleton-in-Teesdale to Sunderland train on 12 September 1957.

5.12

On 15 August 1972, whilst on its way to Ford Quarry, the leading pair of wheels on D5106 (later Class 24) became derailed at the hand points near Claxheugh Rock crossing. 3729 (later Class 08) brought help from South Dock shed to assist in the re-railing.

5.13

NCB 0-6-2T 30 (Kitson 4532/1907) with brakevan, on the way from Lambton Staiths to Penshaw Yard, has just left the Deptford line and is passing Pallion Station on 22 April 1963. This industrial landscape has now largely been swept away.

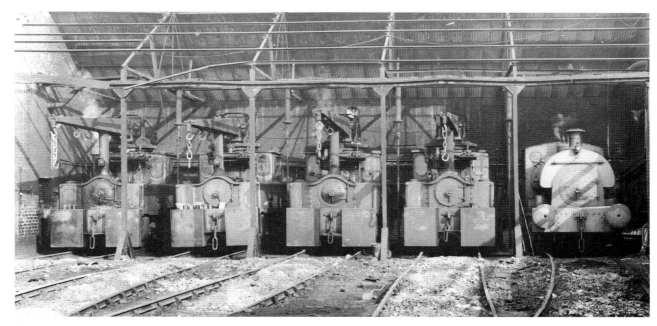

5.14

A connection from the Deptford Branch at Ogden's Lane led to the Doxford Shipyard at Pallion, whose shed provided this splendid line-up of power on 8 April 1969. From left to right are 0-4-0 crane tanks HENDON (RSH 7007/1940), ROKER (RSH 7006/1940), MILLFIELD (RSH 7070/1942) and SOUTHWICK (RSH 7069/1942)- all of which are currently preserved - and 0-4-0 saddle tank GENERAL (Peckett 2049/1944).

5.15

There was no room for a sixth engine in the shed at Doxfords and 0-4-0 crane tank PALLION (HL 2517/1902) often sought nocturnal sanctuary in one of the arches beneath the Queen Alexandra Bridge. It is engaged in clearing-up work at the shipyard on 15 February 1971, four days before rail operations ceased.

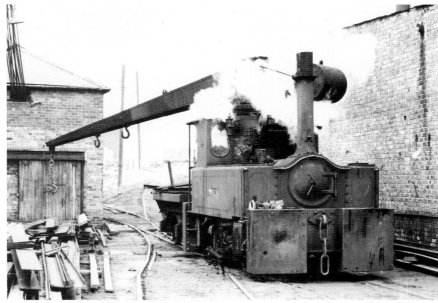

5.16
A Sunderland to Durham Metro-Cammell dmu approaches Pallion on 22 April 1963. NCB 0-6-2T 30 is waiting to come off the Deptford branch and follow the passenger train to Cox Green Junction.

5.17
Bearing a 64H (Leith) shed plate but now allocated to Gateshead 0-6-0DE D3729 (later Class 08) is seen at Deptford Junction with vans for Cornings Glassworks. The severed lines to Lambton Staiths, closed in 1967, are on the right. This photograph was taken on 31 March 1970.

5.18
View from the footplate as NCB 0-6-2T 31 emerges from Deptford Tunnel to arrive at Lambton Staiths with a haul of coal from Penshaw Yard on 9 June 1965. This area is now the Riverside Park.

5.19
0-6-0DE 08176 at the site of Millfield Station (closed 1955). It is about to propel its train from South Dock into the nearby coal depot on 28 August 1981. The view is towards the former Diamond Hall Junction.

5.20
Twenty years after closure to passengers, this exterior view of Millfield Station buildings astride the overbridge in Hylton Road was taken on 11 May 1975.

5.21

At Millfield, Hylton Road originally crossed the railway on the level with the station adjacent to the crossing. The later station was on the overbridge that replaced the level crossing. In this view of 7 May 1966, the Hendon-Pallion route had been converted to a goods line with signal boxes replaced by groundframes. The old station building is on the left; it is now a public house.

5.22

Clayton D8594, hauling a brakevan, approaches Millfield on 26 May 1970. It is on its way to Pallion to work the evening goods to Tyne Yard via South Dock. The bridge in the background carries the Hetton Colliery Railway. This area is now infilled and forms a cycleway/footpath though Metro developments may necessitate its restoration to rail use.

5.23
J39 0-6-0 64833 heads a Blackpool to South Shields express past Burnfield Siding on 5 August 1961. The then closed siding (behind the cabin on the right) had served Robsons flour mill.

5.24
NCB 0-6-2T 10 approaches Fawcett Street Junction (adjacent to Stockton Road) with coal from Penshaw Yard to South Dock on 20 August 1965. The bridges in the background carry Tunstall Road and New Durham Road respectively.

5.25
B1 4-6-0 61014 ORIBI climbs out of
Sunderland to Fawcett Street Junction
(with the South Dock line on the right) at
the head of the 12.54 special to Durham
on Miners' Gala Day, 21 July 1962.
Certain stations in the North-East, whose
regular passenger service had been
withdrawn, were re-opened on Gala Day.

5.26

Larger tender locomotives were unable to turn in the roundhouse at South Dock shed and had to venture far afield for this purpose to the Tile Shed - Harton Junction - Boldon Colliery triangle. Here WD 2-8-0 90434 descends from Fawcett Street Junction to Sunderland Station (a stretch of track closed later in the year) at the start of such a manoeuvre on 12 May 1965. Note the spire of Durham Road Methodist Church.

5.27

View from Park Lane bridge as NCB 0-6-2T 5, blowing-off at the safety valves, drifts down to South Dock with a coal train on 2 July 1964. The former Fawcett Street Station (closed 1879) is on the extreme left and the sea-water pipe to Washington Chemical Works is on the right. The Civic Centre now covers this area and the railway, which had to occupy a tunnel beneath, eventually closed in 1984.

5.28
English Electric 6787 (later Class 37) threads Mowbray Park on a Tyne Yard to Pallion freight and passes over the South Tunnel which it had entered 50 minutes earlier, prior to reversal at Ryhope Grange and again at South Dock, 10 August 1972.

5.29
56077 on the Pallion Branch at Hendon Junction with the late Bob Blackburn in attendance. The line to Ryhope Grange is beyond the signal. 31 July 1984.
The signal box was destroyed by fire on 13 February 1996.

5.30
WD 2-8-0 90445 at Hendon Junction
with the SLS East Durham Limited on
15 May 1965. The line to Fawcett Street
Junction is beyond the location box on
the left, this being at the end of the
former Hendon Station which closed in
1879 upon the opening of Sunderland
Central.

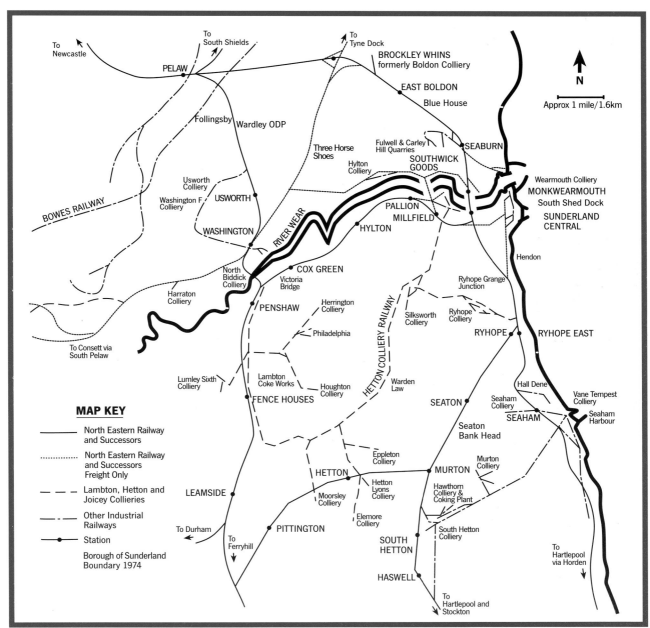

To Newcastle

To South Shields

To Tyne Dock

PELAW

BROCKLEY WHINS
formerly Boldon Colliery

EAST BOLDON

Blue House

Follingsby   Wardley ODP

Three Horse Shoes

Fulwell & Carley Hill Quarries

SEABURN

Hylton Colliery

SOUTHWICK GOODS

Wearmouth Colliery

MONKWEARMOUTH
South Shed Dock

SUNDERLAND CENTRAL

Usworth Colliery

Washington F Colliery

USWORTH

PALLION

MILLFIELD

WASHINGTON

RIVER WEAR

HYLTON

BOWES RAILWAY

North Biddick Colliery

COX GREEN

Victoria Bridge

Hendon

Ryhope Grange Junction

Harraton Colliery

PENSHAW

Herrington Colliery

Silksworth Colliery

Ryhope Colliery

RYHOPE

RYHOPE EAST

To Consett via South Pelaw

Philadelphia

HETTON COLLIERY RAILWAY

Warden Law

Lumley Sixth Colliery

Lambton Coke Works

Houghton Colliery

Hall Dene

Vane Tempest Colliery

FENCE HOUSES

SEATON

Seaham Colliery

SEAHAM

Seaham Harbour

Seaton Bank Head

MAP KEY

─────── North Eastern Railway and Successors

·············· North Eastern Railway and Successors Freight Only

── ── ── Lambton, Hetton and Joicey Collieries

──·──·── Other Industrial Railways

●─── Station

Borough of Sunderland Boundary 1974

HETTON

LEAMSIDE

Moorsley Colliery

Eppleton Colliery

Hetton Lyons Colliery

MURTON

Murton Colliery

Hawthorn Colliery & Coking Plant

To Durham

PITTINGTON

Elemore Colliery

South Hetton Colliery

SOUTH HETTON

To Ferryhill

HASWELL

To Hartlepool via Horden

To Hartlepool and Stockton

N

Approx 1 mile/1.6km

6. HALL DENE TO RYHOPE GRANGE
AND SOUTH DOCK

From Hall Dene northwards to Ryhope Grange Junction the coast route comprises the former Londonderry Seaham & Sunderland Railway (LSSR) of 1854 which conveyed freight to South Dock and from 1855 passengers to Hendon Burn. From its Ryhope East Station, past Ryhope Grange and onwards to South Dock the LSSR ran parallel to the Durham & Sunderland (D&S) line which opened in 1836 carrying coal to Low Quay on the Wear and passengers to Sunderland Moor Station.

In 1858 the Moor Station was replaced by a new station at Hendon and from 1868 this was also used by LSSR trains in place of the Hendon Burn terminus. Hendon Station itself was closed with the opening of Sunderland Central in 1879 when passenger services were withdrawn from the South Dock lines beyond Ryhope Grange. Today between Ryhope Grange and South Dock the Londonderry lines have been lifted and the D&S line singled.

6.1
56116 pauses in the headshunt at Hall
Dene with HAA wagons of coal from the
stockpile at Vane Tempest Colliery,
Seaham, on 4 August 1987. The coast
route lines are in the foreground.

6.2
Hall Dene once boasted a private station for Lord Londonderry who resided at Seaham Hall. Class 141 55540/20 is seen at the crossing on Leeds Neville Hill to Hexham timing trials prior to the introduction of Pacer trains in the North East. The photograph was taken on 26 February 1985.

6.3
An eight mile walk in the early hours was necessary to secure this picture of 43078 SHILDON COUNTY DURHAM leading the Cleveland Executive for Middlesbrough and King's Cross on 31 May 1984. In the still air the HST could be heard starting out from Sunderland Station at 05.49; here it is about to take the reverse curve to Hall Dene.

6.4

Jubilee 4-6-0 45600 BERMUDA skirts the coast and approaches Ryhope East with an excursion to Newcastle from the London Midland Region on 21 May 1961. The sea breeze is causing the exhaust to drift inland.

6.5

V2 2-6-2 60828 with outside steam pipes is seen at Ryhope East with the 16.13 Newcastle to Liverpool train via the coast. 15 August 1960.

6.6
Deltic 9005 THE PRINCE OF WALES'S OWN REGIMENT OF YORKSHIRE nears Ryhope East with the 13.30 Newcastle-Sunderland-King's Cross train on 5 November 1972. It occupies the former Londonderry line. In the foreground is the Seaton Bank line (ex-Durham & Sunderland) with the disused branch to Silksworth diverging on the left.

6.7
45015 has run round the 17.05 Brian Mills Depot to Sheffield parcels at Ryhope Grange on 3 June 1976. It is departing for Newcastle with blue Gresley woodstock BG E70754 next to the engine.

6.8
'Peak' 53 ROYAL TANK REGIMENT
(later Class 45) comes off the South
Dock line at Ryhope Grange with 3J20,
the 17.15 Brian Mills Depot to Sheffield
parcels, on 28 August 1973. The
locomotive bears a wrong headcode.
During the early 1970s, up to four such
parcels trains left Sunderland on Monday
to Friday evenings.

6.9
With double track still in evidence on this
ex-Durham & Sunderland line, Deltic
55016 GORDON HIGHLANDER nears
Ryhope Grange with the 17.26 parcels
train from Brian Mills Depot to Sheffield
on 16 June 1978.

6.10
37513, in Loadhaul black and orange
livery, near Ryhope Grange with a train
of Ferrywagons conveying chipboard to
South Dock on 15 August 1997. At this
location there were once four tracks -
two Londonderry Railway on the
seaward side and two Durham &
Sunderland on the landward.

6.11
20902 LORNA (with 20903 ALISON at
rear) heads south at Grangetown level
crossing with a weedkilling train on
9 July 1996.

6.12
English Welsh & Scottish 37040 near Grangetown level crossing on 17 August 1997 during a Nuclear Electric Fuel Flask Emergency Exercise on the South Dock Branch. The van is being sprayed with foam by the Fire Brigade following a fictitious collision with the train.

6.13
Outside the straight shed at South Dock in 1963, B1 4-6-0 61019 NILGHAI awaits its next turn of duty.

6.14
A wintry 4 January 1965 sees snow-plough-fitted J27 0-6-0s 65853/65835 outside the roundhouse at South Dock shed.

6.15
Q6 0-8-0 mineral engines line up at South Dock Motive Power Depot with the straight sheds in the left background and roundhouse to the right. From left to right the locomotives are 63342, 63367, 63423 and 63456.

6.16
Final day at South Dock Traincrew Depot and Fuelling Point was 9 April 1994. On the left is 56051 ISLE OF GRAIN which was last to leave; on the right are 56081/094. The Welcome Tavern public house is in the left background.

6.17
08888 at South Dock with brakevans TDB 955204/954552 fitted with air brake valves and warning horns for use in leading the train when oil tanks are propelled into the Petrofina Terminal. 31 August 1986.

6.18

60076, in two-tone grey with blue Mainline logo, about to depart Fina plc Sunderland Terminal with oil empties for Lindsey Refinery, Humberside, on a wet, windy Christmas Eve 1997. Roker is visible beyond the river.

6.19

The last industrial line in operation in Sunderland is that of the Port of Sunderland Authority. 0-4-0 diesel 21 (Ruston & Hornsby 395294/1956) was photographed near the Corporation Quay on 1 October 1986. This railway is used as and when required.

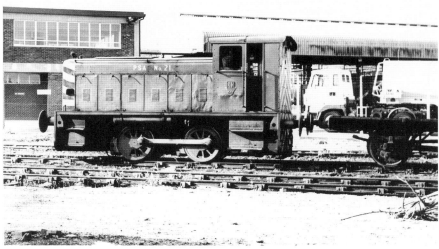

7. SEATON TO RYHOPE GRANGE INCLUDING RYHOPE AND SILKSWORTH COLLIERIES

The railway from Seaton to Ryhope Grange was originally part of the 1836 Durham & Sunderland line which was initially laid out for rope haulage by stationary engines. It included the steeply graded Seaton Bank which descended from Seaton Bank Head to Ryhope Station where it negotiated a sharp curve to run parallel to the LSSR. The D&S lost its passenger service in 1952/53 though for a number of years afterwards it was used for diversions. The final section to Murton stockpile was closed in 1993.

Shortly after Ryhope Station, the former Londonderry branch from Ryhope Colliery (opened 1859) and Silksworth Colliery (1871) trailed in; this was originally connected to the LSSR. Ryhope Colliery closed in 1966, Silksworth in 1971 and the branch succumbed in 1972.

7.1

At Seaton Bank Head level crossing, on 15 February 1992, 56125 begins the descent towards Ryhope with the 11.03 coal train from Murton to Eggborough Power Station. Seaton Bank, once rope-worked and here with track singled, had a gradient of 1 in 42 at one point. The final coal train from Murton stockpile ran on 1 April 1993.

7.2

View from the Houghton to Seaham road at Seaton Nurseries as 37501 descends a 1 in 50 section of Seaton Bank with a rail recovery train, 30 September 1993.

7.3

On 18 May 1993, H.M. The Queen and H.R.H. Prince Philip visited Sunderland which had been created a City the previous year. The Royal Train was stabled overnight on Seaton Bank. Here 47835 WINDSOR CASTLE hauls it past the site of Ryhope Station on its way to Sunderland. 47834 was at the rear.

7.4

47834 FIRE FLY brings up the rear of the Royal Train as it leans into the sharp curve at Ryhope on 18 May 1993 - the location where a Liverpool to Newcastle train was derailed in 1889.

7.5

D286 (later Class 40) and A3 4-6-2
60048 DONCASTER attack the approach
grades to Seaton Bank, near the Toll Bar,
with the diverted 13.00 Newcastle-
Sunderland-King's Cross train on
27 November 1960.

7.6

Heading the diverted 09.13 Newcastle to
York train, A2/3 4-6-2 60524
HERRINGBONE storms away from
Ryhope Grange to tackle Seaton Bank
unaided. It was photographed near the
Toll Bar on 7 May 1961.

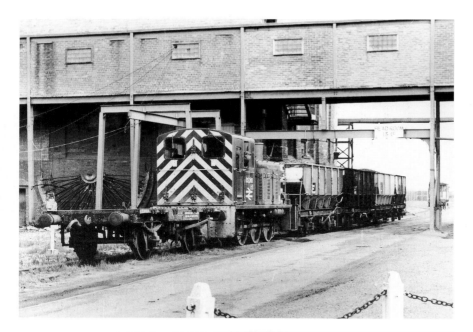

7.7
D2061 (later Class 03) and runner wagon at the closed Silksworth Colliery on 31 May 1972 with coal from South Dock to Hylton Road Coal Depot. This was taken on to its destination by NCB 514.

7.8
D2074/1 (later Class 03) coupled in multiple await departure from Silksworth Colliery with coal for South Dock on 22 October 1971. The pit closed on 6 November 1971 and the area has since been landscaped to include an artificial ski slope.

7.9

A grubby blue D5107 (later Class 24) awaits departure from Silksworth Colliery with coal for South Dock on 21 March 1969.

7.10

J27 0-6-0 65879 removes the rust from the rails as it nears Silksworth with the first train of empty coal wagons from South Dock since the annual colliery holidays. The picture was taken on 21 August 1967 shortly before main line steam from South Dock ceased.

7.11
J27 0-6-0 65865 leaves Ryhope Colliery
(closed later in the year) with a coal train
for Dunston on 28 October 1966.

7.12

J27 0-6-0 65872 leaves Ryhope Colliery
with a haul of coal wagons on
31 October 1966. On the right is
Silksworth box, on the branch to
Silksworth Colliery. The line to
Silksworth Colliery was owned by the
Londonderry Collieries and from 1920
by Lambton & Hetton Collieries, and
finally, by the NCB. It was, however,
worked by main line locomotives after
the Marquis of Londonderry sold the
Seaham & Sunderland Railway to the
NER in 1900.

8. RYHOPE GRANGE TO MONKWEARMOUTH

This link between Ryhope Grange and Monkwearmouth was the Monkwearmouth Junction Railway opened in 1879. It involved construction of the South Tunnel, Sunderland Central Station, the cut-and-cover North Tunnel and the Wearmouth Railway Bridge.

With the opening of Sunderland Central, the former termini at Hendon and Fawcett Street were closed and Monkwearmouth became a through station. The Penshaw Branch, on its way to Hendon Junction, passed over the South Tunnel and a connection from it at Fawcett Street Junction gave access to Sunderland Central. This track was severed in 1965 in connection with layout and signalling rationalisation at Sunderland and the opening of its new signal box.

8.1

A8 4-6-2T 69850 pilots A1 4-6-2 60137 REDGAUNTLET near Spelter Works Road with the 17.00 Newcastle to Liverpool train which was to be diverted via Seaton Bank because of engineering on the coast route on 8 April 1956. Note the lower quadrant distant signal for Ryhope Grange.

8.2

Deltic 55004 QUEEN'S OWN HIGHLANDER unusually finds itself at the head of an evening Sunderland to Darlington football special on 25 August 1981. The train is seen at Villette Road. At one time carriage sidings occupied the space on the left.

8.3

03108 leaves Sunderland Station and approaches the South Tunnel with empty vans destined for the Brian Mills Depot on 30 May 1974. The runner wagon was necessary to activate track circuits.

8.4

Preserved Class 46 diesel D172 IXION emerges from Sunderland South Tunnel with a Bristol to Newcastle special on 27 May 1995.

8.5

As no diesel multiple unit was available, Railfreight-liveried 31252 was working the 14.56 Middlesbrough to Newcastle on 13 August 1985. It is seen arriving at Sunderland Station. This area is now built over and is occupied by shops and commercial premises.

8.6

Sunderland was given TransPennine Express status with the introduction of services to Liverpool via Newcastle on 2 June 1996. On the inaugural day 158801 waits in sidings south of the station to form the 18.45 to Liverpool. Note the Civic Centre on the left and trackbed of the former line to Fawcett Street Junction beyond the train.

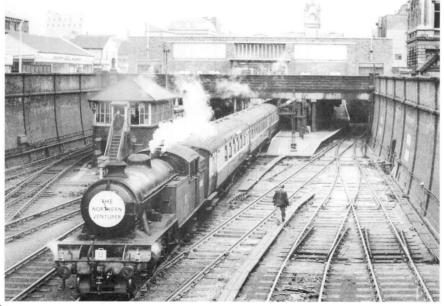

8.7

View from Holmeside bridge as V3 2-6-2T 67688 leaves Sunderland with the Northern Venturer industrial holiday train for Bridlington in 1955.
Note Sunderland signal box and the frontage to the south end of the station which dated from the 1953 rebuilding.

8.8

G5 0-4-4T 67265 awaits departure from Sunderland with the 14.08 to Durham. The 13.55 push and pull service to South Shields is on the left.
6 September 1957.

8.9

At Sunderland's below-street-level station, morning sunshine illuminates Fowler 2-6-4T 42411 which had arrived with the 10.45 from Newcastle on 11 April 1958. The engine was allocated to South Dock.

8.10
G5 0-4-4T 67253 has arrived at
Sunderland with the 18.05 push and pull
train from South Shields on 29 April
1958.

8.11

Deltic D9005 enters Sunderland with the 13.15 Newcastle to King's Cross on 7 June 1964. The train was to travel via Seaton Bank and on the right is a connecting dmu for Seaham. On the left another dmu forms the 13.45 to Newcastle. Note the clock tower and remains of the war-damaged overall roof at the station's north end; the south end was being rebuilt at this time.

8.12

The north end of Sunderland Central looking towards the ticket collectors' boxes and staircases down to the platforms on 7 June 1964. This was the major entrance to the station until 1965.

8.13
Demolition of the north end of Sunderland Station with the North Tunnel cut back to High Street West on 17 April 1966. Littlewoods store now occupies the site on the right. Note the shops with Blacketts in Union Street on the left.

8.14
Sporting LNER green livery, 47522 DONCASTER ENTERPRISE crosses Wearmouth Bridge with the 13.30 Newcastle to Middlesbrough 'Pacer replacer' on 17 February 1988.

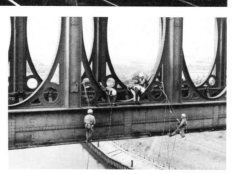

8.15
No scope for the faint-hearted here! Workmen high above the River Wear renew the cradle rail on the Wearmouth Bridge, 23 June 1992.

8.16
One evening the photographer was returning from Newcastle to Sunderland by train. A newly-launched ship was passing beneath the Wearmouth Bridge with a workman at its highest point checking clearance and almost touching the bridge! In this picture 48,000 tonne COLIMA, newly-launched at Deptford, is approaching the bridges in the course of being taken downriver by tugs HOLMSIDER and IRONSIDER.
30 July 1984.

9. HYLTON, SOUTHWICK AND MONKWEARMOUTH RAILWAY

The Hylton, Southwick and Monkwearmouth Railway, always a freight-only line, opened in 1876 from Monkwearmouth to Southwick Junction on the Stanhope & Tyne line near Barmston. It was linked by the Queen Alexandra Bridge to the Penshaw Branch from 1909 to 1921. The HS&MR served Wearmouth and Hylton Collieries as well as industries on the north bank of the Wear. The line west of Hylton Colliery closed in 1926 and the railway was abandoned progressively eastwards as industries ceased to exist or made no further use of rail transport. The closure of Wearmouth Colliery in 1993 sealed the fate of the line.

9.1
A freight train for the Southwick Branch leaves Monkwearmouth Goods Yard behind 0-6-0DE 08176 on 27 February 1981.

9.2
56118 arrives at Wearmouth Colliery to take out the final coal train on 29 November 1993. The train was destined eventually to reach Tyne Coal Terminal. Sunderland AFC's Stadium of Light now occupies this area.

9.3
An ex-Dorman Long 0-6-0ST 3 (RSH 7687/1951) shunts at Wearmouth Colliery on 26 March 1963. Wearmouth was the last colliery in the Durham Coalfield when it closed in 1993.

9.4
31240 heads along the Southwick Branch with a train of scrap from Youngs to Tyne Yard on 21 July 1986. Note the pigeon crees at the top left.

9.5
A cheery traincrew lends interest to this
picture of J27 0-6-0 65887 at Southwick
Goods in 1963.

9.6
08263 with a train carrying steel plates is glimpsed in the shipyard of Austin & Pickersgill Ltd. on 22 August 1983.
In the background is the 1909 Queen Alexandra Bridge whose upper/rail deck became redundant in the 1920s.

9.7
J27 0-6-0 65788 heads a freight between Hylton Colliery and Southwick on 23 April 1963. The right hand track was used by NCB trains. The embankment marks the course of the line from Castletown Junction over the Queen Alexandra Bridge to Diamond Hall Junction near Millfield. The embankment was removed for the construction of Wessington Way.

9.8
NCB 0-4-0ST 11 (Hudswell Clarke
1412/1920) shunts at Hylton Colliery,
Castletown, on 27 August 1969.
This was for many years the western
terminus of the Hylton, Southwick &
Monkwearmouth line which once
extended to join the Stanhope & Tyne at
Southwick Junction.

10. MONKWEARMOUTH TO BLUE HOUSE INCLUDING THE NORTH DOCK BRANCH

From Monkwearmouth the coast route describes a sweeping reverse curve to the vicinity of the former Wearmouth signal box. Here it joins the alignment of the 1839 Brandling Junction Railway from Gateshead whose Wearmouth terminus was near Roker Avenue.
The present Monkwearmouth Station replaced it in 1848.

Just before Seaburn the North Dock Branch diverged seawards for about one mile. This line closed in the mid-1960's.

10.1

The imposing frontage of Monkwearmouth Station photographed in 1998, 150 years after it opened as the new terminus of the railway from Newcastle. It was built in an impressive style to mark the election of George Hudson, the 'Railway King', as an MP for Sunderland. The station ceased to be a terminus after the railway was extended across the Wear in 1879. The station closed to passengers in 1967 and it was reopened as a museum by H.R.H. The Duke of Edinburgh in 1973.

10.2

45053 passes Monkwearmouth with the final 01.15 King's Cross-Leeds-Newcastle sleeping car train on 30 April 1977.

10.3
In Great Western green with brass cabside numberplates and nameplates, 47484 ISAMBARD KINGDOM BRUNEL is seen at Monkwearmouth on 22 October 1985 with a Sunderland to Newcastle parcels train.

10.4
Preserved A4 4-6-2 LNER 4468 MALLARD passes Monkwearmouth on a special from York to the Settle & Carlisle line on 27 August 1988.

10.5
J27 0-6-0 65832 breasts the summit at Monkwearmouth with a northbound freight on 11 June 1965. The Royal Hotel is on the left; it was also designed by Thomas Moore, the architect of Monkwearmouth Station. The hotel's role declined after the station ceased to be a terminus in 1879.

10.6
153315 forming the 09.54 Newcastle to Middlesbrough negotiates the temporary layout at Monkwearmouth where the up (southbound) track had been slewed into the down to facilitate single-line working over the Wearmouth Bridge, which was under repair. On the right, refurbishment work is taking place on Monkwearmouth Station Museum's canopy. 13 August 1994.

10.7
Rear view of the 11.07 Sunderland to Newcastle train on the temporarily slewed track at Monkwearmouth on 13 August 1994. The 'Pacer' nearer the camera is 142019 - one of several in Tyne and Wear livery.

10.8
The 10.30 King's Cross to Glasgow Central IC225 hauled by 47776 and with electric 91026 (pantograph down) bringing up the rear passes Monkwearmouth on a dull, wet 24 August 1997. The train was diverted from Darlington to Newcastle via Dinsdale and Sunderland because of engineering work on the main line.

10.9
37203, in blue Mainline livery, heads an
additional 15.00 Tyne Yard to Seaton-on-
Tees freight through Monkwearmouth on
20 February 1998.

10.10

Spotless V3 2-6-2T 67651 arrives at Monkwearmouth with a special conveying H.R.H. The Duke of Edinburgh on 21 July 1963.

10.11

Following closure by BR, Monkwearmouth Goods Shed was leased by Tyne and Wear County Council for storage and restoration of large exhibits by Monkwearmouth Station Museum Association. This view, taken on 7 May 1977, includes Consett diesel 10 (left) and the North Tyneside electric conductor rail de-icing van (right). Sadly, these had to be moved to North Shields when the goods shed roof was found to be beyond economic repair and the project to develop the shed as a museum had to be abandoned.

10.12
D6788 (later Class 37) with diesel brake
tender propels loaded wagons from
Wearmouth Colliery off the Southwick
branch at Monkwearmouth on 28 July
1970. The goods station, the major goods
depot in the town, is visible to the right of
the semaphore signals.

10.13
40015 (formerly AQUITANIA) at Wearmouth with empty stock off a Newcastle-Seaburn football special on 22 August 1981. The train had previously formed the 08.53 Blackpool North to Newcastle. The football platform, rendered redundant when Seaburn Station opened, was near the cottages beyond the rear of the train.

10.14
A Middlesbrough to Newcastle dmu approaches Seaburn on a snowy 4 December 1976. The North Dock Branch formerly diverged to the left of the rear of the train.

10.15

J27 0-6-0 65887 on the North Dock Branch at its junction with the coast route just south of Seaburn Station in 1963. This particular engine was prone to run hot and was confined to pick-up goods workings at this time. The train comprises brakevan and a coal wagon from Crowder's coal depot.

10.16

J27 0-6-0 65887 on the North Dock Branch near Fulwell Crossing (where tram tracks once crossed on the level) in 1963. Note the stored coaches including an LNER articulated twin. An A4 was once reportedly seen hauling such coaches on the branch. The J27 is superheated with extended smokebox and altered handrail.

10.17

In 1936, on the North Dock Branch
adjacent to Roker Park, the Chairman of
Sunderland Football Club, Sir Walter
Raine named LNER B17 4-6-0 2854
(later LNER 1654/BR 61654)
'SUNDERLAND'. Most of its life was
spent on the Marylebone to Manchester
route and in East Anglia. The engine
was photographed at Liverpool Street,
London, working the 15.36 to Clacton
on 22 February 1957. Note the cast
brass half-football and team colours
beneath the nameplate. The locomotive
was withdrawn from service in 1959.

10.18

The North Dock Branch terminated in rope-worked inclines descending beneath Harbour View to the dock until the 1950s. Armstrong Addison's timberyard, whose products included sleepers and baulks for the railway, is seen on 28 February 1983 with a travelling crane on the internal railway system. It was isolated from the BR network, the North Dock Branch having closed in the mid-1960s. In 1986 Armstrong Addison timber gates and fencing were noted on the Tees Valley Way at Mickleton.

10.19

At first sight the picture suggests that a train crash is imminent at Seaburn on 18 July 1988. In reality Pacer 143002 on the 06.45 Seaham to Newcastle has failed and is being rescued at 08.05 by 143014 which had formed the 07.25 Newcastle to Sunderland. The 07.15 and 07.35 departures to Newcastle from Sunderland comprised diesel multiple units which had to be held back because they could not be coupled to a Pacer.

10.20
Seaburn Station saw use by specials bringing supporters for football matches at Roker Park. On 6 March 1976, 47417 and 46049 arrive 135 mins. late with the 08.15 from King's Cross conveying Crystal Palace supporters who would not reach the ground until half time. The air was thick with Cockney oaths!

10.21
On 12 April 1991, Strathclyde-liveried 156512, which had previously reached Newcastle from Girvan, was pressed into service to work the 11.15 to Sunderland. It is seen here at Seaburn and would work back to Newcastle in time to form the 12.54 to Stranraer Harbour.

10.22
Q6 0-8-0 63400 pounds past Fulwell with a northbound train of mineral wagons in 1963. The sidings for limestone traffic from Fulwell Quarries once occupied the area on the right.

10.23
25090 from Eastfield shed, Glasgow, approaches Blue House with a train from Brian Mills Depot on 18 April 1980.

10.24
4MT 2-6-0 43015 darkens the sky as it passes Blue House with the 14.45 Newcastle to Sunderland train on 12 September 1958. The East Boldon distant signal is on the left hand post and the train has just passed the distant signal for Fulwell box.

And finally

This book began with a look at a wooden wagonway recently excavated by archaeologists. It is appropriate that it should end with a special train on the preserved Bowes Railway, run in connection with a visit by the Association for Industrial Archaeology. 0-4-0 saddle tank 22 (Barclay 2274/1949) stands by the water column at Springwell on a bleak, windy 6 September 1997.

This section of the historic former colliery railway, in the vicinity of Springwell Village, is the City of Sunderland's only preserved line and is shared with Gateshead. The line features steam and diesel traction, rope haulage by stationary engine and the site contains the head of a self-acting incline;

original colliery wagons are in evidence and there is a museum. The railway has recently been extended from Blackham's Hill to Wrekenton and relies heavily on volunteers who are becoming hard to find - these being the lifeblood of the preservation movement.

In order to stimulate interest in trains amongst youngsters of today, Monkwearmouth Station Museum now runs various railway-orientated activities for children - who may hopefully constitute the railway volunteers and customers of tomorrow.